PALM READING

A LITTLE GUIDE TO LIFE'S SECRETS

By Dennis Fairchild
Illustrated by Julie Paschkis

●

RUNNING PRESS
PHILADELPHIA • LONDON

A Running Press Miniature Edition™

Library of Congress Cataloging-in-Publication
Number 94–73868

ISBN 1–56138–626–X

This book may be ordered by mail from the publisher.
Please include $1.00 for postage and handling.
But try your bookstore first!

Log onto **www.specialfavors.com** to order Running Press®
Miniature Editions™ with your own custom-made covers!

Running Press Book Publishers
125 South Twenty-second Street
Philadelphia, Pennsylvania 19103–4399

Contents

INTRODUCTION

We've carried them since birth, but how many of us actually know the lines on our hands? Greek thinkers such as Aristotle, Plato, and Ptolemy saw great significance in these markings and regarded them as valuable keys to understanding character, as did many Roman rulers and intellectuals. Josephus, the first-century Jewish

historian, wrote that Julius Caesar was so skilled in hand analysis that it was "impossible for any man whose palm he had seen to deceive him in any way; in fact, one day, an individual came to him claiming to be Alexander son of Herod, and Caesar promptly recognized him as an impostor with no mark of royalty on his hand."

While modern palm analysts do not recognize a particular marking as the sign of a great ruler, what they read in your hand can give you valuable insights about your life and how you interact with the world.

There are many misconceptions about the practice of palm reading. A short Life Line, for instance, in no way foretells an untimely demise. Modern palmistry is less about predicting the future than about reading a person's character.

This book updates much of the old-fashioned jargon and fated forecasts, and presents the art of palmistry in user-friendly terms. Begin by observing your own hand. Make a photocopy of it. Then do the same with the hands of your friends, family, and coworkers. Note the similarities and differences. Each hand

differs in innumerable ways, but there are—pardon the pun—specific *rules of thumb* for deciphering individual characteristics. These pages will guide you through some of the most important.

Your hand is a miniature map of the inner you. Like maps of the world, everything changes with time—and so do you. It may be impossible to rewrite your past, but it's always possible to break through personal limitations, reassess the building blocks that define you, and re-evaluate who you can be. The keys are in the palm of your hand!

PART I
THE HAND

RIGHT-HAND OR LEFT-HAND DOMINANCE

More than 85 percent of the world's population eats, writes, and works with the right hand. In spite of the achievements of famous lefties such as Leonardo da Vinci, Michelangelo, Benjamin Franklin, Lewis Carroll, and Paul McCartney, old theories about the inferiority of left-handed people persist in our modern,

right-handed world. Modern palmistry dismisses these old ideas but recognizes that left-handed and right-handed individuals have distinct sets of abilities.

Right-handers: You prefer practical, logical reasoning, and tend to be analytical and pragmatic. You always think things through carefully and examine your personal motives before acting. You prefer to play life by the rules and avoid using tactics that would be embarrassing if made public. Be careful: you may be tempted to

relax your ethics when pursuing important personal goals.

Left-handers: You favor intuitive thinking and tend to be more creative, imaginative, and original. You often act on hunches and are not afraid of failure or temporary setbacks because you know these experiences can help you sharpen your abilities. The worst thing you can do is lose faith in your ability to realize your goals and objectives.

Which hand do you read? Palmists look at the left or right hand to read different sets of characteristics. Your

left hand reveals your private side—
your fantasies, hopes, and dreams.
Your right hand shows how you present yourself to the outside world and
how you interact with it on a day-to-
day basis. Regardless of which of your
hands is dominant, you should con-
centrate on the markings and signs of
your right hand for the purposes of
this book.

SIZE

Small hands: If your fingers don't reach past your eyebrows when you rest your wrist on your chin, your hand is considered small. People with small hands see the big picture but often overlook important details. Small hands think big! You are single-minded and powerfully pursue each of your goals with dogged determination. You rely on reason and intellect

rather than intuition. You have the self-discipline to put aside immediate gratification in favor of long-range satisfaction. Most of all, you crave achievement and a steady climb to status and security. A word of caution: your pursuit of professional success may lead you to sacrifice home life and intimacy.

Big hands: Your hands are big when, resting your wrist on your chin, your fingers reach almost to your hairline. Big hands reveal sensitivity, versatility, and curiosity. While small hands skim

the newspaper headlines, large hands enjoy the small print and cartoons. Full of mental energy, you are aggressive about getting what you want but flexible enough to see other points of view. You know instinctively how to reach people on their own terms. You enjoy examining and categorizing others, always asking a million questions. What upsets you most is not having answers, dealing with stubbornness from someone else, and being told that there is only one way to accomplish a given goal.

Medium-size hands: People with medium size hands are good mediators between small and big-handed people. Nimble-witted and responsive, you shrug off problems and setbacks easily. You have a solid core. You pride yourself on being even-keeled and not showing prejudice. You're practical, rejecting what is unsuitable, unhealthy, or unnecessary. You enjoy things that make you feel warm and coy. You seek out serenity, comfort, and the good things of life.

SHAPE

Most palms are a mix of the two primary types. Examine yours closely: one hand shape usually outweighs the other, and provides the key to your character.

Thin palms: The hand with a thin, narrow, rectangular palm is the thinking and feeling hand. You enjoy brainstorming and talking, and have an agile mind. You're bright, quick,

and curious, and your moods change readily. Full of mental and emotional energy, you want to know everything about everybody. You value rationality above all else. When confronted with an emotional crisis, you try to reason things out and make the most logical choice. You tend to push aside instinctive, gut reactions in favor of logical constructs, though your instincts are often right on target.

Square palms: Is your palm square-shaped, like a child's building block? The hand with a square palm is a

practical hand. You take nothing for granted and demand that facts be laid on the table. You possess good reasoning abilities and have a need for security. You shrug off day-to-day upsets and are not easily driven off course. You're a person of action, a hard worker, a doer and achiever. Law and order and no nonsense are your code of honor. You say what you think but may have difficulty seeing other points of view. You can be extremely critical, but you demand no more from others than you expect from yourself. You

have a need to be needed and you derive emotional satisfaction from being productive and useful.

PART II

THE FINGERS

GENERAL CHARACTERISTICS

In addition to examining each finger for specific traits, palmists look at overall finger characteristics to read a more general picture of who you are.

FLEXIBILITY

The degree of flexibility in your fingers tells how adaptable you are. Ideally, fingers should arch gently

backward under pressure. If yours
don't, it might mean you don't like to
admit you're wrong and you refuse to
see the other person's side of the story.
When your fingers flex way back,
arching easily, you'll do anything to
avoid an argument.

LENGTH

No specific measurement defines short
or long fingers. Finger length must be
judged in relation to the length of the
palm itself and is usually gauged by
looking at the back, or fingernail side,

of the hand rather than the front, or palm side.

Very Short Fingers: Your fundamental belief is that you never know what you can accomplish until you try. You have a daring, competitive spirit, and your adventurousness often results in success and recognition. You idealize independence and individuality. Your enthusiasm is contagious and your up-front manner never leaves any doubts about your intentions. Watch out: your exaggerated need to get a job done fast can lead

you to take foolish chances. Aggressive and feisty, you should learn to practice patience and relax.

Short fingers: Do your fingers appear short in relation to the palm? Short-fingered folk decide matters quickly, act fast, and understand the larger scheme of things. Unfortunately, you don't always take time to think matters through. Your abrupt and occasionally reckless actions can have disastrous consequences. Always in a rush, you tend to overlook details. On the other hand, your pioneering

spirit is strong, and no amount of failure can discourage you. Goals that can be achieved quickly are better choices for you than ones that require years of planning.

Long fingers: People with long fingers take their time doing things and tend to fuss over the "Why?" and "How come?" of a job. Planning, analyzing, discussing, and asking questions are important to you. You enjoy examining and categorizing situations. You don't fear compromise or demonstrating affection or other

emotions. Security to you means understanding a situation and having it so well scoped-out you can explain it to anybody else. You have an instinct for putting yourself into others' shoes.

A long palm with long fingers says you enjoy talking things out but may get hung up on small details and miss the big picture. Intuitive and sensitive to others, you're full of empathy. Unfortunately, you frequently put others first, ignoring your own best interests. You're not an aggressive or overly physical person. You work well

in creative arenas. Your ability to grow and expand your field of influence is unlimited. But you aren't looking for glory or prestige—you're content to work behind the scenes. You should look for a career with unlimited growth potential. Routine occupations would deny you the chance to make full use of your creativity and imagination.

A long palm with short fingers signals someone who tends to be argumentative. You often make up your mind before all the facts are on the table. You are impatient with your

emotions and those of others. To you, feelings are stumbling blocks that get in the way of things you want to do. Anger and irritability come easily, but you don't stay mad for long because you want to move on to the next thing. An extrovert, you're well suited to careers that involve change, assertiveness, and adventure.

A short, squarish palm with short fingers belongs to down-to-earth, logical souls who work well in the daily grind of the material world. Preferring a stable and predictable lifestyle, you

dislike change. You're self-sufficient and aggressive about getting what you need. Punctual and straightforward, you see things in an uncomplicated manner and may enjoy careers in agriculture or horticulture, mechanical jobs, and those where you focus on one task at a time.

A short, squarish palm with long fingers reveals someone who is mentally alert, has an insatiable curiosity, and enjoys exchanging opinions and ideas with others. Like a detective, putting together the pieces of a puzzle

amuses you and stimulates your mind. You emphasize level-headed thinking, clear language, and careful research, and you take the time to explain things well. You are intelligent, have no fear of intellectual challenge, and enjoy boisterous, outspoken people. A well-mannered diplomat, you rarely lose your temper and always try to avoid arguments. You weigh your actions carefully and make clear-headed, fact-based judgments, without letting your feelings get in the way. The fields of communication, teaching,

publishing, or public relations are ideal for you.

SHAPE

Thick, fleshy fingers reveal a sensual, erotic, and mostly passive nature. You yearn to touch, see, smell, hear, and taste all that life has to offer. You enjoy good food and luxury, and you may be a bit of a couch potato. But you do want to be productive and transfer your interests into physical form— you may not always be satisfied with admiring the creations of others.

Thin fingers mean that you always take time to think matters out before you act. You weigh the strengths and weaknesses of a situation and make factual judgments without being overly influenced by your feelings. You debate issues cleverly but never become emotionally involved. You are dramatic and creative. A career in communications or working with young people would be a good choice for you, giving you the feedback you need to know you're utilizing your energies effectively.

Knobby fingers with prominent knuckles (not as a result of arthritis) signify strong reasoning abilities. You are a problem solver who thinks logically, taking time to weigh the pros and cons of any action or situation. Large knuckles also suggest objectivity and patience. You don't like disagreements, and because you want to maintain stability in your emotional life, you don't express your dissatisfactions easily.

39

Often success comes to you because you never think about failing.

Smooth fingers with unobtrusive knuckles belong to people who use intuition more than reason. You play

your hunch rather than following conventional wisdom. Your passions usually rule your thinking, yet you rarely act in haste or anger. You often have difficulty asserting yourself and going after

what you want in a direct manner. Because love is vital to your happiness, you place more emphasis on your partner or relationship than on yourself.

FINGERTIPS

Fingertips come in specific shapes, judged from the palm side of the hand rather than the back. Some hands carry more than one shape. Always note which shape is dominant.

Pointed fingertips that taper like a spade toward the end reveal curiosity and a good imagination. A dreamy,

sensitive escapist, you possess a rich fantasy life and enjoy being in love and nurturing others. You'd rather go along to get along. The ultimate peacemaker, your motto might be "Don't make waves." Although not technically artistic, you appreciate music and the finer things of life. You have a wide range of interests and you understand the need to plan for your

POINTED FINGERTIPS

goals to achieve success. For you it's essential to be loved and needed—by a partner, a plant, a child, or a Pekinese.

Rounded fingertips indicate that you enjoy people, are receptive, and react readily to outside stimuli. Rounded-fingertip types rarely like living alone. The constant presence of someone who cares for you makes your world safe and desirable. When you commit yourself in love, you

ROUND FINGERTIPS

43

do so totally and permanently. You are never pushy or forceful, but once you decide you want something you'll exert gentle but continuous effort to obtain it. You should consider careers that require helping others solve their problems: medicine, law, social work, management, or teaching.

Blunt, squarish fingertips are not those of spontaneous folks. "What's in it for me?" is apt to be your song. You gain emotional satisfaction from being careful, orderly, useful, and productive. Your self-reliance and stubborn

determination make
you great in the fields
of sales and industry.
You're a born manager,
skilled at organizing
others and delegating

SQUARE
FINGERTIPS

authority. You crave stability above all
else, often viewing change as undesir-
able or threatening. You enjoy clearly
defined gender roles, job descriptions,
and deadlines.

Spatulate fingertips flare at the
tips and taper toward the knuckles, resembling a cook's spatula or a

Japanese fan. People with spatulate fingertips love physical activity and the great outdoors. You enjoy a challenge and are excited by new conquests. You are vivacious, lively, and occasionally restless. You gain great satisfaction from doing and making things—waiting around for slow pokes or listening to long debates is not your cup of tea. You are hard working and conscientious. You don't need feedback

from others to assure you that you're on the right track—you prefer to work independently.

·——— FINGERNAILS ———·

The fingertips have more nerve endings than any other part of the body. These are shielded by the armor of your fingernails. Fingernails come in all shapes and sizes. Their shape remains fixed from birth and provides clues to personality.

A healthy nail looks smooth as glass, is pliable and elastic, and has a

visible semicircle, or *moon*, at the nail bed. It's said that moons wax and wane, growing larger when you're healthy and keeping fit, and shrinking below the nail bed when your recuperative powers are weaker. A healthy nail is straight or convex, not sunken. The skin beneath should have a rosy pink glow.

Small nails: Nails that are small in proportion to the top third of the finger suggest a person who burns the candle at both ends. You're impulsive, curious, and quick to lose your

temper. Your mind is active and fast. You have difficulty sticking with anything for long. In your rush to uncover facts, you sometimes overlook important details or are careless in your research.

Large nails: Nails that take up lots of the top third of the finger suggest a big thinker. You believe in hard work and enjoy a good challenge. Once you've decided you definitely want something, you're not easily discouraged. Your persistence and single-mindedness frequently bring

you success. You project an image of confidence, vitality, and self-sufficiency, yet you yearn for recognition—and admiration—from one and all. You are strongly sexual and sensual, but you need monogamy and commitment to feel fulfilled.

Thin nails: Nails that are narrow in relation to the fingers reveal folks with penetrating minds. You can focus your attention deeply for long periods of time. Infinitely curious, you're always asking questions. You express your opinions convincingly

and get straight to the point. You're not satisfied with simple facts or superficial explanations—you seek a deeper understanding. Psychology, espionage, or medicine are good fields for you.

Wide nails: Wide-nailed folks make discriminating, practical choices but tend to get argumentative and set in their ways. You have trouble seeing other points of view. You dislike criticism and prefer to do things your way. Security and stability are very important to you. A lover of routine and

schedule, you tend to commit to a job or partner for life.

Oval-shaped nails: Nails that are shaped like eggs are the most common. You are socially minded and take everything in stride. Your passions never rule your thinking—you rarely act in haste or anger. You are acutely aware of what other people think and are inclined to conform to majority rules. You often have difficulty asserting yourself and pursuing your goals decisively. You don't deal well with confrontations, physical or

otherwise. You like to make friends, not adversaries.

Almond-shaped nails: These belong to dreamers, lovers, and sometime martyrs. You enjoy color, music, beauty, and art in all forms, and you like to fill your life with lovely things. Not money-minded, you rarely ask about prices because you hate to deny yourself anything. This often runs you into debt. Highly sensitive, you cannot bear to see anyone hurt (especially yourself). You sympathize readily with the weak and deprived, the underdogs.

Long, rounded nails: These reveal a tolerant, understanding person who often neglects personal needs, putting loved ones first. You prefer to do things with others and enjoy a peaceful home filled with music, art, and laughter. You're the dabbling sort who likes to try anything once. Mentally agile, you learn quickly and enjoy sharing what you learn.

Long nails with squared-off bottoms: People with these nails are less experimental, preferring facts, stability, and predictability. You have trouble

expressing emotions or allowing yourself to relax and let your hair down.
You show concern for others by doing
practical, necessary things.

Square-shaped nails: These suggest
someone who needs a life that runs with
logic, schedule, and clockwork precision. You're a lover of routine, order,
and common sense. You plan carefully
for the future and make certain that
everything you do is built on a solid
foundation. You perform your duties
efficiently and modestly and derive a
sense of satisfaction from helping others.

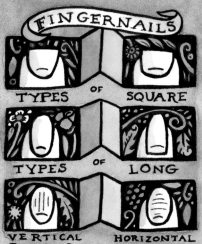

Small, squarish nails: People with these nails tend to dominate conversations. You seek recognition by expressing yourself dramatically. Your style is forceful and energetic. You can be very charming, but you are also self-centered and have trouble recognizing opinions other than your own.

Vertically ridged nails: Nails with visible ridges or indented ripples running from nail bed to fingertip flag the worrywart. Your emotions are confusing and you tend toward high anxiety. Your compassion and need for

love make it difficult for you to draw the line with dependent people. A dreamer, you're often so carried away by your fantasies that you forget the mundane world of paying bills and performing day-to-day tasks. You are highly critical of yourself.

Horizontally ridged nails: Horizontal ridges, or *gutters*, across the nail suggest weak recuperative powers and melancholy. Easily hurt, you fear nothing you do will make things better and you often give up without trying. Try talking things out with

others; reach out more and you may be pleasantly surprised.

• ——— FINGERPRINTS ——— •

Like the stripes on zebras and the crystal patterns in snowflakes, no two fingerprints are exactly alike. Fingerprints form five months before you are born and grow with you, but their original pattern never changes. There are three basic types, which account for approximately 80 percent of all prints.

These patterns represent the most basic, unchangeable elements of your

personality. Each hand may carry more than one pattern. In looking at your hand, note which pattern is in the majority. Also, some fingers may carry *composite fingerprints*—a blend of two or more patterns. In such cases, note the dominant image.

The Loop: The loop fingerprint resembles a cowboy's lasso. If you have a majority of loops, you're adaptable, agreeable, and you don't like to rock the social boat. You thrive on social interaction and maintain a large circle of associates and acquaintances,

WHORL

LOOP

ARCH

speaking with them frequently and staying in touch with those who live far away. You make the most of every situation, but you're concerned about what others think and sometimes have difficulty expressing your true feelings or opinions.

The Whorl: The whorl looks like the bull's-eye of an archer's target and is the sign of an individualist. Self-expression is important to you and you especially enjoy exploring new ideas and concepts. Conventional wisdom and accepted truths don't hold much

water in your book—you're eager to contest them with original ideas of your own. Even when your ideas and dreams are grandiose or unrealistic, you refuse to believe they're impossible. Something of a flatterer, you're charming and very interested in romance.

The Arch: Looking like an upside-down capital letter "T," the arch is commonly found on the fingers of efficient, hard-working, and reliable people. Your mind works in an orderly and organized fashion. You take

nothing at face value, dissecting everything to see what makes it tick. You
have a good memory for facts, figures, and words. Your keen analytical
ability makes you ideal for fields like
auto repair, accounting, book editing,
computer programming, or research.
Cautious and conservative, you tend
to be more of a follower than an intellectual pioneer.

THE FIVE FINGERS

Each finger of the hand is named after an ancient mythological deity or one of the planets in the heavens, and each tells a different story.

• JUPITER: THE INDEX FINGER •

Jupiter reveals your assertiveness and leadership abilities.

Long: The index finger is long when it rises above the nail bed of the

middle finger. This suggests star quality and strong self-confidence. You test your own limits and believe firmly that you never know what you can accomplish until you try. You take pride in yourself and your achievements. You're tough to ignore when you have something to say, have a strong sense of self, and always seek new ways to do things.

Average: When the index finger is nearly the same length as the ring finger, you enjoy being in control. You possess a strong sense of the dramatic

and can be flamboyant in the way you express yourself. You tend to magnify your emotions and have a taste for the larger-than-life.

Short: When the index finger is shorter than the ring finger, you prefer to follow rather than lead. You gain emotional satisfaction from being helpful and you like to feel needed. You prefer not to be the center of attention or have too many responsibilities. You're extraordinarily sensitive and can be hurt easily. This may sometimes lead you to take a back seat to others.

Conservative, traditional, and spiritual, you are inclined to follow established philosophies and faiths. You can't stand to see any suffering. Your keen sensitivity enables you to feel a kinship with all living things.

• SATURN: THE MIDDLE FINGER •

Saturn reflects how you learn things and how disciplined you are.

Long: A long, straight, and proud-standing middle finger reveals a love for schedules. You're serious about your commitments and don't mind being

alone. Work is very important to you and you're happiest when situations are orderly and structured. You possess natural managerial abilities and are known for shrewdness, diligence, and reliability. Although you are ambitious, status and recognition are not as important to you as honor and personal happiness.

Short: Middle fingers are considered short when they only reach the top of the ring finger. You tend to be old-fashioned and conservative, and you like to stick to what you know

rather than take chances on new ideas or practices. You hold on to your resources and prefer to make it on your own, never relying on others. Taking risks is difficult for you.

Curved: Bent or curved middle fingers are the sign of a collector, one who hoards and saves things. Your physical home and personal belongings represent security and stability to you. Highly critical of

CURVED SATURN

yourself, you might be inclined to undervalue your abilities.

Large knuckles: Middle fingers with pronounced knuckles say that learning and scholarly pursuits are your greatest skills. You have plenty of common sense about finances but have trouble with mundane things like remembering where you left your keys. You're defensive about your rights and sometimes fear that your independence will be hampered by authority figures or too many laws. People are impressed with your ability

to assert yourself, and they admire the way you defy any rule that interferes with your desires.

Spatulate tip: When the tip of the middle finger is spatulate, you have a love of the outdoors, gardening, and science. You're very close to your

friends and feel a strong bond with nature and animals. You have no desire to behave aggressively, tend to be withdrawn, and may have difficulty asserting yourself. Even so, you're a staunch defender of equal rights and fair play.

•—VENUS: THE RING FINGER—•

Venus speaks of your personal style, capacity for joy, happiness with work, and appreciation of the arts.

Short: A straight ring finger reaching above the nail bed of the middle

finger says that you don't fear show-ing your feelings. Caring for someone makes your world safe and desirable.

Average: When your ring finger is slightly longer than your index finger, you crave recognition and approval. You take pleasure in money and the things it can buy. You communicate well with color, fashion, and visual cues. You like crowds, sharing your thoughts, and being in the limelight.

Long: Watch your checking ac-count balance if the ring finger is *much* longer than the middle. Your

eyes are bigger than your bank book when it comes to money management. Once you've established a relationship, it's likely to endure—a long ring finger is a good sign for business partnerships and love interests. You are willing to work hard to make a relationship strong and lasting.

• MERCURY: THE LITTLE FINGER •

Mercury deals with how you communicate and learn.

Long: A little finger that reaches above the ring finger's top knuckle

reveals that you think big and talk well. Optimistic and adventuresome, your enthusiasm is contagious. You learn quickly and demonstrate an eagerness to get things done. Long little fingers make for fine speakers, singers, and musicians. You may have more ideas than you realize for changing social values and inspiring others. Follow your heart.

Square-tipped: A square-tipped little finger says that you speak well, state your case clearly, and are skilled at argument. You could be a good

judge, umpire, or lawyer because you act from a sound sense of equality and fairness. Be careful to keep your ethical standards high.

Spade-tipped: People with pointed tips on their little fingers are full of warmth and charisma. You are conservative, don't like causing friction, and are inclined to do what is expected of you. At best, you're open-minded; at worst, vacillating and overly accommodating. You have trouble asserting yourself, perhaps because you don't want anyone to think you're uncoop-

erative. Friendship and approval are your highest priorities.

Bent: A little finger that bends away from the hand suggests an inability to get along with people. Your focus on details often causes you to miss the larger picture. If you relax and realize that everyone has failings, you'll improve your chances for satisfactory relationships and a good financial situation.

•— URANUS: THE THUMB —•

Uranus tells of your sense of individuality, determination and perseverance,

open-mindedness and willingness to change, and sense of self-worth.

Long: A long thumb reaches up to the middle joint of the index finger. This is the sign of a strong ego and a healthy sense of self. You're always ready with a word of encouragement and feel genuinely joyous when making people happy. You feel secure in a commanding position. You seem never to grow tired and frequently burn the candle at both ends. Pride keeps you from becoming overly dependent on others.

Short: A thumb that doesn't reach the bottom of the index finger says you're short on willpower and follow-through. You have problems making up your mind. It's difficult for you to separate yourself from others' needs and desires. Too compassionate, you don't know how or when to draw the line with people who cling to you. You're easy to get along with, but you've got to learn to say "no."

Waisted: A thumb with a noticeable *waist*, tapering between the knuckle and the palm, suggests an ability to

WAISTED THUMB

understand peo-
ple, animals, and
plants. You have
boundless curio-
sity and a desire
to expand your
horizons. You seek to enhance the
monotony of daily life with fantasy
and entertainment. You're easily dis-
tracted and you must occasionally
discipline yourself to stay on course.
You have a talent for dealing with
small groups and inspiring them to
achieve excellence.

Flexible: If the tip of your thumb arches freely backward, you do what others tell you and are overly concerned about what the neighbors think. Your heart rules your head and you may have trouble making rational decisions.

Stiff: An inflexible, stiff-tipped thumb makes you argumentative and overly set in your ways. You pride yourself on getting the job done, but you like to get it done your way. You rarely take chances with time or money. Your friendships may be few, but they are usually forever.

Thick: A thick, sausage-looking thumb belongs to those who shun the limelight and prefer working behind the scenes. Your mind works in a carefully calibrated, disciplined, and orderly fashion. You enjoy trouble-shooting and correcting errors. You learn best by repetition and applying knowledge in some practical way. You would do well as a mechanic, accountant, or researcher.

Stiff and thick: A thick and inflexible thumb belongs to someone who prefers working in structured, imper-

sonal, and unemotional environments. Cautious and conservative, you are inclined to stick with tried-and-true methods. Beware of becoming a workaholic: learn to balance work with play. Stop worrying about problems that never happen.

Wide angle: Does your thumb naturally fall away from the fingers, "shunning" them? A 45-degree or larger angle between your thumb and the side of your hand reveals a generous, open-minded person willing to compromise and consider the options

for all concerned. Ideas and concepts are important to you. You respect intelligence and individuality but are more concerned with theory than application. Your quick wit and humor make you very charismatic. You make the most of opportunities to demonstrate your creative talents, but you do so without alienating competitors. You assert yourself positively when you encounter resistance to your plans. Your understanding of people and their problems offers numerous opportunities for professional success.

Narrow angle: When the space between your thumb and the side of your hand is small, with the thumb hugging the fingers, you don't like to do things spontaneously. You're goal-oriented and like to have plenty of time to plan your moves carefully. You're a good judge of character and your understanding of people gives you advantages in realizing your personal and professional objectives. You feel that most difficulties can be resolved through good communication. People with problems depend on

you because they know you can show
them how to make better use of their
time and resources.

• THE MOUNT OF APOLLO •

The fleshy elevation below the thumb
is called the *Mount of Apollo*. Like
its mythological namesake—the sun
god—it speaks of personal warmth
and high energy levels.

A solid, high, and rounded Mount
of Apollo suggests someone who is
generous, possesses an enthusiasm for
life, and recovers quickly and easily

from illness. You're a rugged individual with an innate sense of drama. You enjoy personal attention, you're well informed, and people seek out conversation with you. Because you like people and have a talent for dealing with them, you might consider a career in education, communications, or management.

A flabby or sunken Mount of Apollo says that your mental

MOUNT OF
APOLLO

stimulation comes from within, from your emotional core. You are inclined to think a great deal about ways to make yourself feel secure. Your cautious and meticulous nature enables you to excel at tasks that require attention to detail and precision. You derive a sense of satisfaction from being able to help others. Be careful not to neglect your own needs when others come looking for handouts or sympathy.

A flat Mount of Apollo means you yearn for consistency and security. You prefer to surround yourself with

people who think the way you do. Watch out for those who try to intimidate you. Take a firm stand when you know you're right. Don't feel obligated to others who try to take advantage of your compassionate nature. Establish goals that are within your abilities and stop doubting you'll be able to achieve them.

PART III
THE LINES
OF THE PALM

GENERAL CHARACTERISTICS

Each palm is different and carries a variety of shapes and lines. Lines can change, lengthen, or disappear over time. Hands may broaden or shrink. When you're angered or upset, your hands redden and sweat. If you're sad or withdrawn, they turn pale.

There are a few guidelines when looking at palm lines. In general, the

more lines, the more emotional the individual. Palms with very few lines tell of a more physical, practical, organized spirit. Fine, thin lines signal someone who is more intellectual and creative. An excess of fine lines suggests nervousness and scattered energy. Deep, wide, well-etched lines mark someone with strong likes and dislikes. Chained, feathery, or broken lines are found in the palms of those who don't like being alone and have a fragile self image.

THE MAJOR LINES

The three main lines—the Life, Head, and Heart Lines—appear on nearly every palm. The Life Line begins at the wrist near the base of the thumb and curves around the Mount of Apollo to the edge of the palm, ending somewhere between the thumb and index finger. The Heart Line runs across the palm near the base of the fingers. The Head Line

stretches across somewhere between the Heart and Life Lines.

● —— THE LIFE LINE —— ●

The Life Line doesn't reveal how long you'll live, but speaks of your enthusiasm for life and willingness to enjoy and fight for what you want and love.

A deeply etched Life Line, free of breaks or tassels, assures a robust and fruitful life. You are a high-energy person who embraces challenge and opportunity. Affectionate and physically demonstrative, you enjoy life and

of a flatterer when it suits your purposes. Social, outgoing, and extremely communicative, you talk to anyone who'll listen and see every conversation as an opportunity to grow and prosper.

One or two deeply etched lines that only take up the upper half of the palm suggest personal happiness, good imagination, and an appreciation of the arts. You understand the larger picture and have a fantastic imagination. Your middle and later years will bring success and happiness.

Venus Lines that start low on the thumbless side of the palm and end below the ring finger predict help from family. You're attentive, affectionate, and loyal to those you love. Your early conditioning was important in your rise to prominence. Be careful not to fall into ruts and routine. Whatever career you choose, be certain you have enough room to grow and develop to your fullest.

A multitude of Venus Lines suggests that, although you may have your fingers in many financial pies,

you'll eventually succeed on your own merits and individuality. You assimilate information easily and are knowledgeable about a wide variety of subjects. You make the most of circumstances to further your ambitions by using your well-developed creative imagination and versatility.

MERCURY LINE

The Mercury Line, also known as the *Hepatica*, runs from the base of the palm to the fleshy area below the little finger. Like the Saturn Line and

Girdle of Venus, this line is absent in many hands.

If the Mercury Line is a series of broken or wavy lines, hastiness, impatience, and indigestion are likely. You always have several things going on simultaneously and may have trouble limiting yourself to one job or relationship. Your interests are many and diverse; almost anything can attract your attention for a brief time.

One straight, clear Mercury Line says you keep matters in perspective, know how to have a good time, and

never take life too seriously. You are optimistic and gravitate to healthy life choices, rarely allowing depression, nervousness, or worry to overpower you. Your highly developed social skills and your ability to discipline yourself will allow you to enjoy many advantages.

•— THE AFFECTION LINES —•

Modern palmists do not believe that a future marriage, in the sense of a legal union, can be foretold by scanning hands—nor can the number of

AFFECTION
LINES

children you'll have
be determined. Mar-
riage is an institution
established by the
church and state—it
is not the sole form
of love or deep emo-
tional commitment that can come into
people's lives. For this reason, the lines
that were once referred to as *Marriage
Lines* are now called *Affection Lines*.

Affection Lines are small horizontal markings located at the edge of
the palm between the base of the little

finger and above the Heart Line, running parallel to the Heart Line.

When one or more of your Affection Lines is deeply etched, you're capable of strong, sincere affection and lasting friendship. In relationships, you are mostly concerned with permanence and fidelity. Quality, not quantity, is important to you in affairs of love. You think and talk a great deal about relationships, and are inclined to romanticize one-to-one attachments. Your sensitivity requires a partner who has a sympathetic nature.

One deep Affection Line supported by strong Heart and Head Lines speaks of a yearning for stability and equality in relationships. You have a knack for understanding others and are generous and affectionate with those you care about. You understand implicitly how to please your partner. Generally, you are on good speaking terms with all your acquaintances. People tend to be open with you because they feel you really care.

When Affection Lines are faint, chained, or broken, you are cautious

about love commitments and a bit self-critical. It's difficult for you to assert yourself in relationships. Believe more in yourself and don't set your expectations unrealistically high.

When Affection Lines are chained or possess a number of downward slants, be alert to dependency issues or feelings of inadequacy with those you love. Think about the goals you hope to reach in your unions and make achieving them your most important priority. You are the only one who can build substance in your life. Don't be

afraid to let others know how you feel, even if they disagree.

Double or parallel Affection Lines suggest compassion for others. Preoccupied with the present, you should learn to plan ahead and invest the time and energy needed to derive the maximum yield from your love of people.

When no Affection Lines are evident, relationships or marriage may be more for convenience or etiquette, not love. Preoccupation with social standards may cause you to shelve your personal interests or pleasures in

deference to what others think. You're basically well integrated, but your success in love affairs may be delayed if you are not willing to roll up your sleeves and give it everything you've got.

It's impossible to tell precisely when love and happiness will occur, but the general rule for centuries has been that when Affection Lines are close to the Heart Line, you will find emotional satisfaction early in life. When they're close to the base of the little finger, you'll be a late bloomer.

Now you've got the keys to reading some of life's secrets in the palm of your hand. Use your new skills to enrich your life, examine your character, and reassess who you want to be. As the proverb says, "Running water is beautiful water. If you dam a river it stagnates. So be a channel."

strive for security and independence, and avoid relying on others.

You have a strong need to be needed when the Saturn Line curves away from the thumb and toward the little finger. Be more aggressive in promoting yourself and your ideas, and don't be afraid to let others know you won't allow them to use you. Live up to your potential and capitalize on your resources to achieve financial security. Avoid making comparisons between your life achievements and other people's success.

A Saturn Line made up of two or more lines, clear or broken, marks someone who works best in partnerships, both romantic and business. You're good at organizing others. Cautious by nature, you take time to plan your moves carefully, but you adjust quickly and learn new skills or methods when necessary. Basically honest and sincere, you win the respect and confidence of friends and fellow workers easily. Many of your tests and financial hurdles involve home and family.

When a Saturn Line, or a forked branch of one, starts within the Life Line, your physical home is your source of security and stability. A traditionalist, you hold tightly to conservative opinions. You prefer to do things the way Mom and Dad did. Gaining financial and emotional security is a high priority for you. When you have this marking, you're likely to benefit from inheritance or financial assistance from relatives. Make certain there is always room to expand in your career, because once you get

started, you won't be content until you fulfill your maximum potential.

A Saturn Line ending at the Head Line says you have trouble separating your emotions from rational thinking. Although you have strong ties to your family and a deep sense of responsibility to them, you recognize the importance of standing on your own. Your sense of humor may save you from experiences that would otherwise leave you emotionally crushed.

A Saturn Line that stops at the Heart Line urges you to have more faith in

yourself. Life hassles are likely to be due to a poor choice of partners and lovers. Your thoughts often center on what other people think. You have a deep need to relate to others, professionally and socially, and you derive great satisfaction from indulging those around you. Knowing you've been helpful makes you feel good, but you need to remember to look out for Number One!

Public success or recognition from peers is in your future when the Saturn Line veers toward the index

finger. Because you're adventurous and believe you can succeed, you probably will. You have a talent for getting people to open up to you and reveal information, and you may some day find this useful.

•——— VENUS LINES ———•

Lines traveling upward from the middle of the palm to the ring finger are called *Venus Lines*.

One long straight Venus Line is best, suggesting career brilliance. You can be quite charming and something

MINOR
LINES

don't leap into love affairs blindly. Once you commit yourself in love, you desire nothing less than a complete merger with your partner.

A chained or broken Heart Line says many of your relationships are more like romantic or casual friendships than deep emotional unions. While it is admirable to help those who deserve it, be on guard against people who would abuse the privilege and use you as a doormat.

A Heart Line that travels straight as a ruler across the palm says you devote

a lot of time to thinking about the best ways to realize your dreams. You have a deep drive to win. People appreciate your dedication to service. You have no taste for dramatic emotional displays and you rarely remain angry for long. Although you're flirtatious, you're also calculating, viewing love as a cool business deal.

A wide space between the Heart and Head Lines reveals a need for

independence. You aggressively seek out whatever life has to offer and are willing to take chances that might scare away the more cautious. Something of an evangelist, you eagerly express your own views and philosophies. You have a low tolerance for slow pokes and deadbeats, people who cling to you or smother you. You seek partners who are able to fend for themselves. You act aggressively in romantic relationships and become easily offended if rejected. Regardless of your age, you're a child at heart.

HEART

HEAD

MERGING LINES

Be careful not to act like a spoiled brat when you don't get your way. Aim for compromise, not confrontation.

When the Heart and Head Lines merge into one as they travel across the palm, you have trouble making decisions. Your attention span is short

and your interests many—you often start things but fail to finish them and sometimes you promise more than you can deliver. A sucker for flattery, you constantly seek reinforcement from friends, family, and lovers. Remember to treat others as you'd like them to treat you.

THE MINOR LINES

Every palm differs in the number and nature of its minor lines. Here are some of the most common.

•— GIRDLE OF VENUS —•

Any series of U-shaped or horizontal lines above the Heart Line and below the middle and ring fingers constitutes what is called the *Girdle of Venus*. If your palm carries this mark, your sex

drive is strong and you have a hearty appreciation of physical and sensual pleasures. You have a rich fantasy life and are keenly aware of what others think. Power is important to you, but you prefer wielding it behind the scenes. You stay on top of current events, what's hot and what's not. You enjoy the arts and music, and are curious about how others live.

GIRDLE of VENUS

You're emotionally dramatic, especially
when in love. If you practice modera-
tion in everything you do, you'll have
many rewards and will be surrounded
by people who love you.

• —— SATURN LINE —— •

The Saturn Line, also known as the
Fate Line, is found in only 40 percent
of all palms. It is composed of two or
more vertical lines running upward
from the wrist to the middle finger,
frequently veering off course between
the Head and Heart Lines. Saturn tells

how you feel about the material world and economic opportunities.

When clear and straight, a sense of contentment with the material world and daily structure prevails. The urge to acquire dignity and become self-sufficient in your work environment commands much of your attention. Your emotional poise allows you to win over adversaries.

Broken, split, or faded lines denote a desire for money and recognition. You put a great deal of energy into acquiring the necessities of life. You

structure and stability you provide to family and coworkers.

A Head Line ending in a tassel-like fork—called a *writer's fork*—shows that you're versatile, curious, and inventive. The wider the fork, the more adaptable and resourceful you are, with an ability to bring a breath of fresh air into stale, stagnant situations.

• —— THE HEART LINE —— •

The Heart Line serves as your emotional barometer and tells about your affection and feelings for all of the

people in your life, not just for your lovers or life partner.

A deeply etched Heart Line means you see a role for yourself as a peacemaker. Even if you have no particular talent for the arts, you enjoy most art forms. You place great emphasis on home and family—your ties to family members are strong, whether or not your experiences with them are positive. Because you take everything personally and want everyone to get along, you are likely to interpret differing opinions as attacks or criticisms

of you. Still, you're basically an optimist. People often turn to you for guidance because you show that you're sensitive to their needs.

A faint Heart Line says that you require special attention and enjoy being pampered. Your heart rules your head, and your opinions and ideas are colored by your feelings and emotional attachments. You don't like being alone—you function best in partnerships. You want everything about your relationships to be nice all the time, and you can't tolerate anger or arguments.

The Heart Line is considered long when it reaches to just below the index finger. This is the sign of the romantic. You are protective, nurturing, and devoted to friends and loved ones. You don't like being alone, and you devote much time to pursuing and maintaining your relationships with others.

A short Heart Line travels only halfway across the palm and says that no one takes love, sex, and relationships more seriously than you do. Passionate and playful, sensual yet sensible, you

This book has been
bound using handcraft methods,
and Smyth-sewn to ensure durability.

The dust jacket and interior were
designed by Paul Kepple.

The text was edited by Brian Perrin.

The text was set in Granjon,
Greco Deco, and Coronet Script.

people. You're known for your courage, energy, and desire to win.

Breaks and disappearances in a Life Line say that you probably spend more time in contemplation than in taking action. You owe it to yourself to be more assertive. You may feel your role is more one of helping others to

BREAKS & TASSELS

lead, but you must learn to assert your own ideas, too. Don't be so fearful of taking risks or taking charge. Consider serving the public through social work or helping the mentally impaired or physically handicapped.

When the Life Line makes a wide, sweeping curve across the palm, you're a magnanimous, sunny individual, generous to fault. You relate well to children and enjoy helping those in need. You enjoy being heard, respected, loved, and seen as strong and reliable. You give freely of your time and money.

You enjoy each day and want to explore new horizons and ideas.

A Life Line beginning high under the index finger denotes a need for acknowledgment. Your ego is high, your ambition large. The ultimate individualist, you can't bear to have someone tell you what to do or how to do it. You're combative and energetic, but may have trouble disciplining yourself and focusing your abundant energy. Although you enjoy praise, it's almost impossible for you to accept advice or acknowledge mistakes.

When a Life Line hugs the thumb closely, you shy away from the spotlight. You enjoy helping others and tend to think more about the greater good than of your own wants and needs. Although you may not be willing to stand up for yourself, you often fight for the rights of others. More mental than physical, you're short on vitality, requiring a lot of rest when ill.

•—— THE HEAD LINE ——•

Your quality of mind and intellectual appetite is what the Head Line

is all about—not your IQ or membership in Mensa.

A short Head Line that doesn't pass halfway across the palm suggests a one-track mind, shortsightedness, and being closed to new ideas. You have a penchant for order and are very conservative and self-centered. Issues of power and control are likely to play a role in your life. You assume authority easily and take well to decision-making roles.

The longer the Head Line, the greater your perceptive abilities and

dedication to learning. You respect knowledge and believe in equality. You're strongly opinionated, but never tire of learning new things. You enjoy companionship and have many friends. You sometimes overestimate your abilities, but your willingness to learn and quick wits take you far. Writing, teaching, public relations, or public speaking are good professions for you.

A faint or broken Head Line or one that resembles a linked chain means you're disorganized and have a wandering mind. You lack the organzation

and perseverance to see projects through to completion. You're open to new ideas, but you insist on being free to do things your way. As a result, you sometimes distance yourself from companions and coworkers. Your life will be greatly enriched if you set aside your fears and anxieties and work to help those who cannot help themselves.

The deeper the Head Line, the more you harness your wits and put your know-how to good use. Optimistic and idealistic, you always look for the silver lining and believe things

will turn out for the better, if not the best. Talkative and gregarious, you enjoy sharing ideas with others and have the ability to organize and inspire groups of people.

If your Head Line travels straight and level across the palm, you're a just-the-facts, cool, and logical type. You hold stubbornly to your beliefs regardless of what others think. Clear thinking is your credo. Serious and at times pessimistic, you can become terribly critical of abstract or revolutionary ideas.

When the Head Line takes a sharp upward bend toward the little finger, you use your wits for making money—lots of it! You rarely say anything you're sorry for later. Time is money and you get things done while others dream on. Your no-nonsense attitude helps you in all fields and endeavors.

A Head Line curving gently downward to the wrist denotes good imagination. Lacking attention for mundane matters, you drift in and out of conversations and your mind seems